# How To Successfully Day Trade On Robinhood

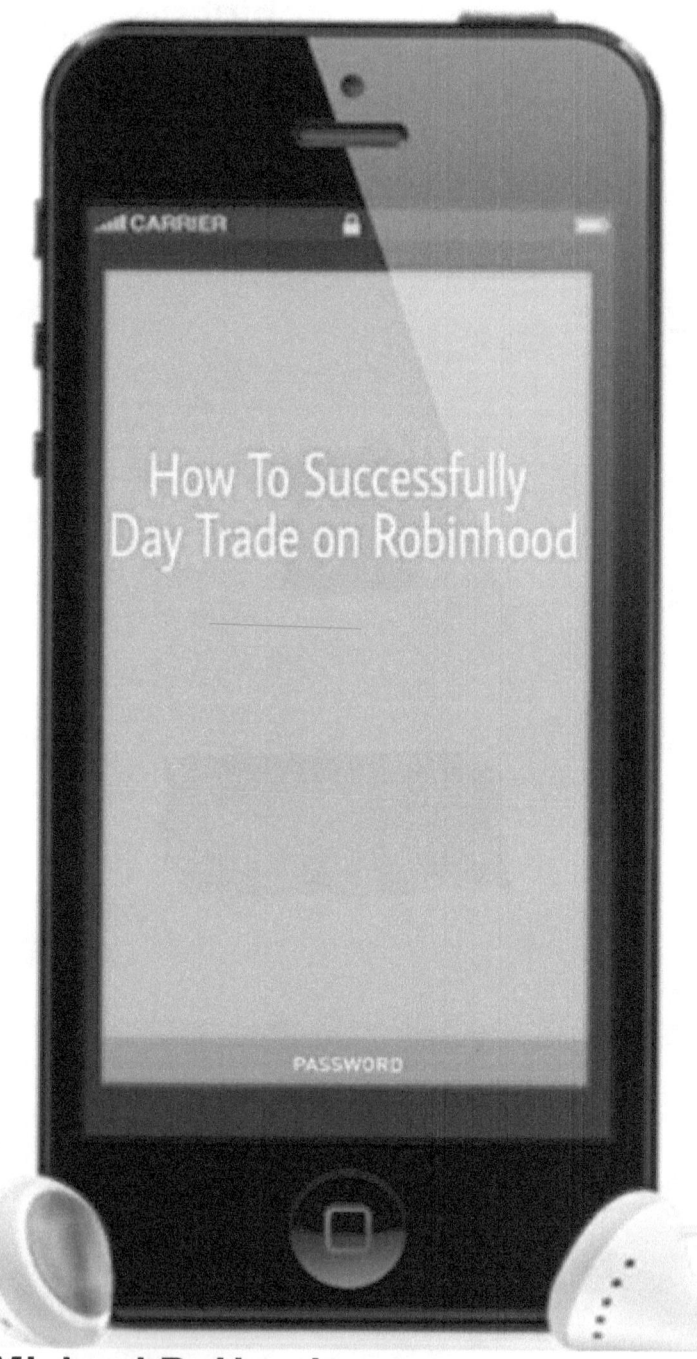

**By Michael D. Henderson**

**RISK WARNING**

How To Successfully Day Trade on Robinhood offers general trading advice that does not take into consideration your own trading experiences, personal objectives and goals, financial means or risk tolerance. If you have any concerns, it is suggested that you seek advice from a professional financial advisor. Keep in mind that past performance is no indication of future results.

## Copyright

How To Successfully Day Trade on Robinhood by Michael Henderson Published by DGTO LABEL Swamp Road, Doylestown PA 18902

© 2018 Michael Henderson

All rights reserved. No portion of this book may be reproduced in any form without permission from the publisher, except as permitted by U.S. copyright law. For permissions contact:

dgtolabel@gmail.com

Cover by Michael Henderson

Ebook ISBN:

## Copyright 2018 Michael Henderson, All Rights Reserved

Disclaimer

Last updated: May 07, 2018

The information contained in on Trade Day Successfully To How Robinhood(the
"Book") is for general information purposes only.
Michael Henderson )the" Author ("assumes no responsibility for errors or omissions
in the contents in the Book.
In no event shall Michael Henderson be liable for any special,

direct, indirect, consequential, or incidental damages or any damages
whatsoever, whether in an action of contract, negligence or other tort,
arising out of or in connection with the use of the Book or the contents of
the Book. Michael Henderson) the" Author ("reserves the right to make additions,
deletions, or modification to the contents in the Book at any time without
prior notice.

# Table of Contents

Personal letter to my reader….pg.5

Why I Love Robinhood….pg.8

The MDH. Story….pg.10

Chapter 1: Day Trading Basics….pg.13

Chapter 2: Risk Management….pg.15

Chapter 3: Choosing the Right Stocks….pg.18

Chapter 4: How Much Money Do I Need To Day Trade….pg.23

Chapter 5: Intraday Chart Patterns (When To Buy, Sell, Or Not Buy At All)….pg.28

Chapter 6: How To Trade With Scanners….pg.35

Chapter 7: Trade Management and Trading Psychology....pg.36

Chapter 8: Creating a Trading Plan....pg.39

Day Trading tools....pg.42

Glossary....pg.44

## My Personal Letter To My Readers

Dear Friend,

Before I say anything about trading, first let me say thank you for purchasing my book. As an token of my appreciation I'm going pay it forward and give you this 11-digit code 67564757325. Use this code at this site www.wstgt.com/67564757325 and you will be able to get a vacation at a discount to these locations: Orlando, FL, Williamsburg, VA, Las Vegas, NV, Gatlinburg, TN, Myrtle Beach, SC, Cocoa Beach, FL. Mostly everyone likes to travel so I figure why not help out. Now onto the trading stuff.

The thing that makes making money a rewarding and joyous activity is that when God blesses you with more than enough of it you can become a blessing to those less fortunate than you. But, in order to do that you must have an understanding that all the money everywhere belongs to God and you're just being steward over the portion he gave you. But this point of view depends on your relationship with the greatest gift God has ever given human society and that's Jesus Christ.

So as I got ready to publish this book I felt it wasn't complete unless I gave you the opportunity to accept Jesus Christ as your Lord and savior. What that means is you believe 2000 years ago Jesus died on the cross for you that you might be saved. This is so important I couldn't ignore it. For me to teach you about day trading and not share Jesus Christ with you in a moment in time that will never happen again between you and I would be wrong on my part being a disciple of Christ.

Furthermore, there is a link between being successful financially and the application of biblical principles about money. In fact, it's been said that Jesus talked more about money than faith and prayer combined. And one of his biggest concerns was not you having money but your relationship with it.

> I Timothy 6:10
>
> *For the LOVE of money is a ROOT of all kinds of evil. Some people, eager for money, have wandered from the faith and pierced themselves with many griefs.*

Jesus, even went as far to teach us what to do with money and became angered when we mismanaged it.

> *Matthew 25: 14-30*
>
> *Again, it will be like a man going on a journey, who called his servants and entrusted his wealth to them. ¹⁵ To one he gave five bags of gold, to another two bags, and to another one bag,[a] each according to his ability. Then he went on his journey. ¹⁶ The man who had received five bags of gold went at once and put his money to work and gained five bags more. ¹⁷ So also, the one with two bags of gold gained two more. ¹⁸ But the man who had received one bag went off, dug a hole in the ground and hid his master's money.*
>
> *¹⁹ "After a long time the master of those servants returned and settled accounts with them. ²⁰ The man who had received five bags of gold brought the other five. 'Master,' he said,*

'you entrusted me with five bags of gold. See, I have gained five more.'

²¹ "His master replied, 'Well done, good and faithful servant! You have been faithful with a few things; I will put you in charge of many things. Come and share your master's happiness!'

²² "The man with two bags of gold also came. 'Master,' he said, 'you entrusted me with two bags of gold; see, I have gained two more.'

²³ "His master replied, 'Well done, good and faithful servant! You have been faithful with a few things; I will put you in charge of many things. Come and share your master's happiness!'

²⁴ "Then the man who had received one bag of gold came. 'Master,' he said, 'I knew that you are a hard man, harvesting where you have not sown and gathering where you have not scattered seed. ²⁵ So I was afraid and went out and hid your gold in the ground. See, here is what belongs to you.'

²⁶ "His master replied, 'You wicked, lazy servant! So you knew that I harvest where I have not sown and gather where I have not scattered seed?²⁷ Well then, you should have put my

*money on deposit with the bankers, so that when I returned I would have received it back with interest.*

*28 "'So take the bag of gold from him and give it to the one who has ten bags. 29 For whoever has will be given more, and they will have an abundance. Whoever does not have, even what they have will be taken from them. 30 And throw that worthless servant outside, into the darkness, where there will be weeping and gnashing of teeth.'*

So before we go any further, let's get you into right relationship with God so he can help you get into a right relationship with money. The bible says if you confess with your mouth the Lord Jesus and believe in your heart that God has raised Him from the dead, you will be saved. Please repeat this aloud:

> *9 that if you confess with your mouth the Lord Jesus and believe in your heart that God has raised Him from the dead, you will be saved.*

Father God, I am a sinner in need of savior. I believe you died on the cross for me, so I confess with my mouth that you are Lord Jesus, and I believe in my heart that you rose from the dead, and for that I shall be saved…Amen.

Grace and Peace

Mike H.

## Who Cares What The Naysayers Are Saying? Here's Why US Little Guys Love Robinhood

When I first got into investing and learned about day trading, it really irked me that unless I had at least $25,000 available to deposit most brokers (if not all) wouldn't allow me to open an account. Most books I read on finance instructed me that if I wanted to become wealthy I needed to have my money working for me. Day trading interested me but why in the world would I need $25K to get started. Apparently, the thinking behind this rule is if an investor doesn't have the necessary 25K to get started then he/she probably doesn't have the financial stability or intellect to really trade within such volatile markets.

Today, is new day. Brokers such as Robinhood and others like it have leveled the playing field for the little guy, the one who doesn't have 25K laying around to throw at stocks. And though many of the robust features at big name brokers aren't available at Robinhood, things like hot keys for entering and exiting trade positions fast, great phone customer support (recently, they've introduced 24/7 requests callback phone support), technical studies within charts, and even the ability to change the way charts are displayed (besides the two settings within the platform – candle and lines), Robinhood is still a Godsend.

Robinhood users can open an account with very little start up cash, choosing between maintaining a cash account or margin account if the user can maintain a balance of $2,000. These funds can be used for long term investing, day trades, cryptocurrencies and even swing/options trades and all this can be done from the convenience of a mobile device. And if you are not mobile friendly you can shoot over to your laptop and trade with Robinhood from your computer.

But, and this is a BIG BUT, the greatest feature of Robinhood in my honest opinion is the ability to buy and sell stock commissions free which is trend that has spread to almost every financial brokerage firm. And, as of this writing another one of my favorite brokers now offers commission free trades. Their name is TD Ameritrade on the think or swim trading platform. Maybe, I'll talk more about them later. But anyway, that's right, Robinhood does not charge a commission when you take trades. This is by far my favorite thing. Let me explain why this is so valuable to us little guys. Let's say you open 2 trading accounts with $500 (which some brokers allow you to do nowadays) one at Robinhood and the other at some other broker that allows those kinds of minimum deposits and they charge at least $5.00 commissions per trade and you jump into day trading. Here is the magic of Robinhood:

> *If you see a stock you like trading at $2.50 per share and you buy 100 shares in each account here's how you win with Robinhood and lose with the other broker. $2.50/share times 50 shares = $125.00 and as day traders we know prices fluctuate very fast so we try to capture profits quickly from 5 to 10 cents from our entry price (in this case – 2.50). In our scenario, the stock price increases to $2.60 and we sell our shares in both accounts and take our profits. Within Robinhood we*

*walk away adding $5.00 to our account bring our balance to $505.00. But within the other broker we end up taking a loss because of the commission structure. When we bought and sold our position it cost us $5 each way ($5 to buy and $5 to sell) so, instead of our balance increasing, it decreases because we only made $5 on the trade but it cost of $10 to complete the trade bringing our balance $495.00. Additionally, if the stock price dropped to $2.40 our Robinhood balance would be at $495.00 but the other broker account balance would be $485.00, a $15 loss. The $10 it cost to complete the trade and $5 we lost in the trade.*

Can you see why now WE LOVE ROBINHOOD!

## My story:

My day trading story like many other professional day traders began with a lot of excitement about the potential to make hundreds, thousands or even tens thousands of dollars from trading stocks. But not soon after I began I was met with frustration, lots of hard earned money lost and much self-talk about why can't I make this work. But I'm getting ahead of myself. First, let me tell you why I got into day trading in the first place.

## DGTO

Some years ago I founded and created a clothing company called DGTO (originally - Da Gospel Take Ova) now known as (Dear God, Take Over). The company was promising but was never able to reach its full growth because of many factors, but largely because of lack of capital. I never liked the idea of borrowing the money from the bank because I knew I would need a significant amount of money to really get the business off ground which (could) would put me debt. And, if my business failed then how would I pay back the money that I borrowed. So this raised the question "How do I get enough money to fund my business?" That's when I found day trading. Through much internet research I learned of the ups and downs of day trading and decided I was going to use this to fund my business. Now, I just needed to learn how to do it. I read a couple of financial articles and watched a few YouTube videos but I still felt pretty illiterate about the subject. I also noticed quite a few people selling "how to" courses on day trading but they were pretty pricey and I wasn't totally convinced that if purchased one of those courses that I would learn what I needed to be successful at day trading. After watching some more YouTube videos and much mental tug of war about whether to buy or not buy an online day trading course, eventually I gave in and made a purchase. For $1500 I bought a "how to" day trade online course and began studying the material.

## Thank God I Bought That Course

I was very pleased with the course. I thought after reading those articles and watching those YouTube videos that I had a sufficient knowledge base on the subject. Nothing could be further from the truth. If I would have started trading money in the stock market before having bought and study that online day trading course I would probably have fell in a worst financial situation than I did. Read the next line twice and aloud: **In DAY TRADING YOU HAVE THE POTENTIAL TO LOSE HUNDREDS OR THOUSANDS OF DOLLARS IN SECONDS**. So educate yourself BEFORE you begin.

## Trading with Real Money

The day finally came when I felt I was ready to day trade. I followed the instructions on how to open and fund a day trading account and I began trading. I can still remember like it was yesterday. I took two trades, finished green on both of them and made $68. I couldn't believe how easy it was to make money in the stock market (so it seemed). The next day full of excitement I tried trading again but this time I wasn't so lucky. I lost more money than I made the previous day and finished the day red. That eventually became my trading pattern, small green days and large red days until my account was out of money. For the next few months the pattern continued. I would take money from my savings account put it into my trading account and weeks later the money would be gone. Frustrated, and no closer to achieving my goal of funding my clothing company I gave up and learned an expensive lesson...day trading was hard.

## Quitters Never Win, and Winners Never Quit

In the following months I stepped back from the stock market and only traded once in a while on my phone on the app Robinhood and with very very small position size. So small that if I had a green day I probably made a $1 and on a red day probably lost $2. I was trying to learn how to trade profitably because what you can do with small position size, you can eventually do with large position size. Plus, I kept feeling like I knew I had the ability to trade successfully.

I pulled out the day trading course I purchased and went through the material again. Consequently, there were things I didn't understand completely before that now were more clear. Things like strategy development, risk management, profit/loss ratio, trading metrics, and mental stops. All these things I saw previously but because of my anxiousness to jump into trading and "start making fast money" I kind of breezed through them and really didn't grasp the full understanding of them. So, I take a few weeks re-studying the course and really absorbing the key concepts of day trading and prepare to take another shot at day trading stocks. This time I changed to a different broker (Robinhood), funded my account and began trading.

At first, things didn't seem much better than the first time around but because I was tracking every trade I took I was able to determine where I was making errors in my trading. After careful analysis I discovered what I needed to do to start winning and winning big. I put together a strategy to use the edge I had discovered to see if it would work and like a charm it did. I began to finish green every day I traded and as of this writing my longest consecutive green day hot streak is 15 days. This strategy (and variations of it) that I developed, that I use every day in the market are the ones I'm going to share with you in this book. But first, you must know what is day trading and how to do it. So let's start there.

## Chapter 1: DAY TRADING BASICS

**What is day trading?**

Day trading is the buying and selling of shares of a stock intraday (same day). For example, if a person buys 10 shares of XYZ company for $4.00 a share at 10 am on October 20, 2017 and sell those 10 shares at 10:30 am on October 20, 2017 regardless if price went above $4.00 or below $4.00 during that 30 minutes this is considered a day trade. If the person were to sell those shares after October 20, 2017 regardless of the time the trade would no longer be considered a day trade. This information is important because the SEC (Security Exchange Commission), the entity that regulates trading has specific rules for day trading versus long term investing and everyone who day trades has to abide by them.

## Can You Day Trade?

The answer to this question is yes. But, a more relevant question to ask is should you day trade? And the answer to that is maybe. Successful day trading requires a unique set of skills and disciplines not native to the average person and until these skills and disciplines are developed then no, you should not day trade.

## Day Trading 101

As a beginner trader there are a number of things you need to know. There are two phases of trading: 1. Strategy development and 2. Trading your strategy. As a new trader (especially on Robinhood) your focus should definitely be on strategy development because entering the stock market without a strategy makes being a successful day trader difficult and if you ask some people they may say nearly impossible. With statistics showing that 9 out of 10 day traders fail, you need set yourself up for success. Here enters the first tool you'll need to familiarize yourself with -- paper trading.

## What is paper trading?

Paper trading is the activity of using fake money to purchase shares of stock. The purpose of this is to help new traders familiarize and participate within the stock market in real time without the risk of losing real money. With the market being as volatile as it is, paper trading helps you test and develop trading strategies until you are confident enough in your strategy to make the jump to trading with real money.

But there is a caveat and I can definitely attest to this. Trading with fake money and real money will have entirely different emotions. Let me show what I mean. Let's say you are trading in your paper trading account and just realized you earned a profit of $5000 from selling your shares of a stock in five minutes. You might get excited that you were right about that particular stock but the excitement may not last as long knowing the profit was all fake. But let's say you lose $5000 in real money in 3 minutes and if you don't hurry and sell your shares of this stock you could lose more money. $5000 might turn to six, seven, even ten thousand dollars. Anyway, you eventually sell your shares for a lost of $5500. All the emotions you may feel I can't even describe here but one thing is sure you will feel hurt. This is why it is important to understand that paper trading has its place in the strategy development phase but it can never entirely replace trading live with real money.

## Chapter 2: RISK MANAGEMENT

Of all the topics discussed within this book, understanding risk management and the role it plays in you becoming a successful day trader is hands down the most important. Within day trading risk takes on many forms and you must familiarize yourself with each one.

**Exposure Risk** - This is the length of time your within a trade. Day traders normally don't stay in positions no longer than five minutes or even less. They get in then get out, hopefully taking profits with them. In my experience the best trades usually go in the direction you expect it them go ( whether that's up for long positions or down for short positions) immediately after you enter them. If that doesn't happen there's no need to keep holding the trade--GET OUT! Then look for another set up.

**Distance between Stop loss vs. Profit Target Risk** - This is the gap between the price point where you entered the trade, the price point where you expect the price to go and the price point where you plan to exit the trade if it unexpectedly doesn't go in your favor. The better you are at this the more successful you'll be at trading. **You must have good entry points**, anticipating the point where the stock will break out because no day trader ever is quick enough to capture a stocks entire upward move. And if you are getting in too late you'll be getting in when a stock is on its way down (Or up for short positions though as of this writing Robinhood doesn't offer shorting) costing you to lose money.

For example: let's say you get into a trade at $2.25 (Price where you entered) and you set for yourself a ten cent profit target of $2.35 (The price point where you expect the price to go and you'll sell your position and take your profits). You'll also want to set a stop loss target of ten cent at $2.15 (price point where you plan to exit the trade, sell your position and take the loss if it unexpectedly doesn't go in your favor). This distance between your stop loss and profit target is the distance between stop loss vs. profit target risk.

Talking about profit and stop loss makes this a good place to mention profit loss ratios. This is your average winners against your average losers. In order to be a profitable day trader you need to consistently trade with a positive profit loss ratio. Most successful traders aim for a 2:1 profit loss ratio. In other words, whatever they are willing to risk in loss, they stand to double that if they profit. They'll risk $0.10 in order to make $0.20.

Using the example from above, let's say you get into a trade at $2.25 (The price where you entered the trade) but this time instead of setting a ten cent profit target of $2.35, you set a twenty cents profit target of $2.45, (The price point where you expect the price to go) and a ten cents stop loss at $2:15 (The price where you'll at sell at if the trade goes against you).

The reason for this is to operate at a 2:1 profit loss ratio. Risking one dollar to make two.

What you don't want to do is consistently trade at a negative profit loss ratio like 1:2, risking two dollars to make one dollar.

To help you see the importance of profit loss ratio here's some stats to remember:

2:1 Profit loss ratio = 33% accuracy is break even

You have to right about your trades 33% of the time to break even

1:1 Profit loss ratio = 50% accuracy is break even

You have to be right about your trades 50% of the time to break even

1:2 Profit loss ratio = 66% accuracy is break even

You have to be right about your trades 66% of the time to break even.

**Max Loss** - Your max loss is the maximum amount of money your willing to lose in a single day before you stop trading for that day. Always have a max loss.

For example: If your max loss is $1000/day once you lose $1000, regardless how many trades you've taken or didn't take yet and whether its 9:31am and the trading day just started or its 3:30pm and its close to the end of the trading day, YOUR DAY IS DONE. Rest your emotions, take a step back and clear your head. But, ill be the first to tell you that this is easier said than done.

# Chapter 3: CHOOSING THE RIGHT STOCKS

Selecting winning stocks can be very challenging and almost impossible when all the possibilities are considered. Everyday there are literally thousands of stocks within the market to choose from and tons of information on each one. So how do you choose the best stocks to trade?

Without a good framework for choosing good stocks you're simply looking for a needle in a haystack. I'm going to give you the exact strategy that I use for choosing stocks. This strategy has help me grow my account to where it is now since I began trading a couple years ago.

First thing you're going to need is a stock scanner. There are several out there to choose from, free and paid versions. I use this every day to help sift and sort through the thousands of stocks available on the market. Prior to trading, I set the scanner to search through the entire market and find stocks that meet a certain criteria that I set within the scanner. Once the 9:30am opening bell rings the scanner starts compiling a list of stocks that meet the certain criteria I've set within the scanner.

Now, instead of looking through thousands of stocks to choose from, I'm now looking at 10 or 15 potential stocks to trade that day. To further narrow my stock search I look for the stocks that are showing a lot of price action and steadily moving upward. Once it moves up at least 40 to 45 cents for penny stocks and $2.00 or $3.00 for expensive stocks (stocks priced above $25.00) and close to making a new "high of the day" price I pull up its charts and level 2 (within the Think or Swim trading platform) and start getting ready to make my entry and take the trade.

Here are the criteria I use within the scanner:

- Low Float - Under 20 million. (Scarce supply often times causes heavy demand)
- High Relative Volume - 2x times its normal average
- Price range - $1.50 - $25.00
- % change - Up at least 4%

Here are my criteria for determining whether to take a trade:

- Low float (under 20 million)

- High Relative Volume (2x times it normal average)
- A former runner based on daily chart and previous intraday moves
- No moving average resistance on the charts, especially the daily chart.
- Volume spiking around time of entry
- Strong daily chart with the price above 200 EMA and no resistance nearby
- News or technical breakout driving the momentum

## HOW TO READ STOCK CHARTS

Stock charts contain a lot of information, most of which you will not need to know to be a successful day trader. Having said that, I'm going to show you what information I look for when I read stock charts and I'm day trading on Robinhood.

Once a stock's price starts gradually moving up hitting new highs I quickly pull up the charts on this particular stock. You must do this fast because the stock may be setting up for major move upwards and you want to give yourself a chance to get a good entry point. Once the charts load up I have In front of me the daily chart (which shows the stocks performance over the last 52 weeks), the 5min chart (which shows the stocks intraday performance within 5 min intervals), and the 1 min chart (which shows the stock's intraday performance within 1 min intervals).

But stock charts can display a whole lot more information than just timed interval intraday performances. Some of the technical analysis (sometimes called studies) charts can display are:

    Volume weighted average prices

    Percent change

    Bollinger bands

    MACD

    Relative Strength Index

By no means is this a comprehensive list and to compile a list here of all the studies available within stock charts is outside the scope of this book. But this should give you an idea of what's available to you.

Within my charts the technical analysis I use are exponential moving averages; the 9 EMA (The average price of the last 9 price changes), 20 EMA (The average price of the last 20 price changes), 50 EMA (The average price of the last 50 price changes), and 200 EMA (The average price of the last 200 price changes).

Additionally, I have the level 2 up (This shows how many shares are being bought or sold as it happens) showing for the stock. This helps me determine whether the stock price has room to squeeze up higher or not. When a stock is moving up swiftly all it takes is for one or two sellers with huge position (share) sizes to form a invisible ceiling at a particular price point which will prevent the stock from going higher until those shares are bought up by buyers. And if there isn't a lot of buyers the stock won't get past that price (It takes buying to push the price up). This is very noteworthy information because if you decide to buy the stock at that price point where the seller(s) have formed a wall, chances are you'll have to sell your position at a loss because the stock price will fall from where you bought it at with slim chance of going back up at that time.

After quickly reading the level 2, the first chart I look at is the daily chart because within that chart I have the 9, 20, 50, and 200 EMAs and if the current stock price falls below any one of those moving averages chances are I won't trade it. But…. And this is a BIG BUT, if the current price is above three of the moving averages and just below the last one and the stock is showing signs of strength upward I'll keep the stock on watch. Reason being, in day trading moving averages are usually considered lines of support (A place where the stock's current price is having a hard time dropping below) or lines of resistance (A place where the stock's current price is having a difficult time climbing above). So I keep the stock on watch because if it breaks pass the final moving average stocks tend to squeeze up 30 to 50 cents or more. And depending on how many traders were watching as it climbed it may climb $1 to $2 and that's what us day traders like to see.

The next chart I look at is the 1 min chart. I'm checking the candlestick pattern to see if the stock is strong or weak to the long side, and if it is forming a pattern that indicates whether its a good time to buy this stock. The reason for this is because I know thousands of other traders are seeing the same thing I'm seeing and if the stock is showing signs of strength they're looking for an opportunity to profit (just like me) from this price activity.

Next, I check the five minute chart to confirm what the 1 minute chart is showing. If the five minute chart is showing me a red candle forming but the 1 minute chart is still showing a green candle forming I won't buy the stock. The five minute chart is such a good chart to get a good feel as to what the buyers and sellers are doing and since a red candle is forming it means that stock is set to reverse and now I have to wait for it to consolidate and set it up again, which may not happen that same trading day.

But if the stock is still in play because the 1 minute is showing strength and green candles forming and the five minute chart is showing strength and green candles forming, I start to watch the level 2 closely for huge position size sellers as well as the 1 minute chart to see about taking the trade and getting a good entry point. This is the nuts and bolts of my trading strategy and we'll get into the full details of it in chapter 5.

# Chapter 4: HOW MUCH MONEY DO I NEED TO TRADE?

To answer this question without confusing you I need to explain the difference between a cash account and a margin account. A cash account is an account where only the amount of money you put into the account is available to trade with it. A margin account is an account where you put in your own money to trade with but the additional benefit of this type of account is your broker lends you money on top of what you put into the account (This additional money is called leverage). Giving you more money to trade with.

In a cash account you can trade as much as want until your cash runs out and every trade you take takes 3 days to settle. What does that mean? Here's an example:

> Let's say Danny has a cash account with XYZ broker with $2500 In the account. He sees a stock he wants to buy and the price of the stock is $4.00 per share. Danny puts in an order to buy 300 shares at 9:40am on Monday, February 2, 2018. This transaction will cost Danny $1200 (300 shares x 4.00 = $1200). At 9:43am the stock price is at $4.50 a share so Danny decides to sell his 300 shares for an $150 profit (0.50 x 300 = $150). Danny's cash account balance is now $2650 ($2500 + $150 = $2650) but because trades take 3 days to settle in a cash account the rest of trading day on February 2, 2018 Danny only has $1300 left to buy stocks. That additional $1350 won't

*become available to trade with until Thursday, February 5, 2018. The huge downside to this is if the stock price continues to rise (let's say to $5.00) Danny wouldn't be able to buy 300 shares no more because those 300 shares now would cost him $1500 ($5.00 x 300 = $1500) and Danny only has $1300 left in his cash account. He could buy less than 300 shares but I think you get the picture here.*

A lot of traders with small accounts don't particularly like cash account because of the 3 days to settle rule (though some brokers have a two day settle rule). I, on the other hand I'm familiar with a cash account because I used to use it everyday and in some respects I like it more than a margin account and here's why. Within day trading your emotions can easily get the best of you (Yes, this has happen to me) causing you to lose focus of your strategy and begin trading with frustration and anger, also called revenge trading. Especially after you just lost a ton of money. But with a cash account even if your emotions are running circles around you on a particular day and you continually keep taking bad trades, eventually you will run out of cash in your cash account forcing you to take a step back and gather yourself. Cash accounts have built in brakes to help keep you from speeding to financial ruin.

In a Robinhood margin account the money used to purchase a stock becomes readily available to buy another stock after you the sell the initial stock. And you can do this as much as you like long as you meet the minimum $25,000 financial qualification. What does this mean?

Within a Robinhood margin account as I stated earlier they give you leverage and it varies between 1k, 1.5k, and 2k based on how much you are willing to pay monthly. This means if you put $2500 in your Robinhood account and you upgrade it to a margin account and you choose the 1k level upgrade you now have $3500 available to you to day trade with. But, because you only deposited $2500 and haven't satisfied the $25,000 minimum, your account is subject to the United States PDT (Pattern Day Trader) rule. This States that you are only allowed 3 trades within a rolling 5 day period. For example:

> *Let's say Danny has a margin account with XYZ broker and he initially deposited $2500 into his account. His broker gives him 1k leverage so Danny has $3500 to buy and sell stock. So, on Monday, February 2, 2018 Danny sees a stock he wants to buy. The price of the stock is $7.00 per share. At 10:05am Danny places an order to buy 200 shares of this stock. The transaction will cost Danny $1,400 ($7.00 x 200 = $1,400). At 10:09am Monday, February 2, 2018 the price of the stock is still $7.00 so he decides to sell his 200 shares for no gain or loss. At 10:20am Monday, February 2, 2018 Danny sees another stock he likes at $3.00 per share and decides to buy 300 shares. The transaction will cost Danny $900 (3.00 x 300 = $900). At 10:27am Monday,*

*February 2, 2018 the stock price has fallen to $2.80 and Danny decides to sell his shares for a loss of $60 (0.20 x 300 = $60).*

Now there are a couple of things I want point out about this example that will help differentiate between a cash account and margin account. In this example, after Danny completed his first trade his money was readily available once the trade was complete to buy more stocks. Margin accounts make this possible because of instant settlement. Also, Danny could buy a lot more shares because of the leverage he received from his broker making his potential to gain profit greater but also increasing his potential to lose greater as well. Furthermore, because Danny never deposited the minimum of $25,000 Into his margin account so his account is subject to the United States PDT rule. And after taking those 2 trades (buying and selling is one trade and Danny did this twice) Danny is only allowed to buy and sell stock one more time between Tuesday, February 3, 2018 and next Monday, February 9, 2018 because the

PDT rule States you are only allow 3 trades within a rolling 5 day period unless you satisfy the $25,000 minimum balance within your margin account. And if Danny had the minimum $25,000, he could have traded as much as he like and not have to worry about the PDT rule. But if Danny was careless and wasn't paying attention to how many trades he had taken already and took more than 3 trades, Danny would get a margin call on his account from his broker. This means Danny now owes his broker $25,000 or bring his account up to a $25,000 balance by the end of the trading day.

Fortunately, within the United States most brokers won't even let you open an account unless you have $25,000 to deposit. But, for those of us who don't have that kind of cash to shell out brokers like Robinhood give us a chance to trade within the market.

Going back to the original question which began this chapter "How much money do I need to trade?" it all depends on which broker you choose you to open an account with. Just remember, in a Robinhood cash account you decide how much you want your initial investment to be. To open a margin account, just remember for United States based brokerage firms you will need a minimum of $25,000 if you want to avoid the PDT rule.

Having said that, those who are still willing to take a stab at day trading must first educate themselves on day trading (reading books like this, investing in other available resources, listening to seasoned traders share their knowledge, etc.) because then and only then will you know how much you want to put in to get started and that's the bottomline.

## Chapter 5: INTRADAY CHART PATTERNS (WHEN TO BUY, SELL, OR NOT TO BUY AT ALL)

Buying and selling stocks is the name of the game and anybody with money can play. But buying and selling at the right time, choosing the right stocks and becoming a profitable Robinhood day trader is the part of game it seems only a 10% of traders win at. The other 90% of traders fail daily.

As you read this chapter I want you to keep in mind the information you read within chapter 3 because it goes along with it.

After the opening bell rings and the trading day begins thousands of traders are looking and waiting patiently (or anxiously) for the right set up to form. These forms take the shape of particular and popular chart patterns. Robinhood user can see these patterns if they switch fromf the default line patterns to the candlestick chart patterns within the application. But, I also advise Robinhood users to use another charting software while you are trading on the Robinhood app. I use the Think or Swim platform which is free and can be easily downloaded. Anyway, these patterns help traders determine when a trading opportunity is in front of them and you should be no different.

There are 4 particular chart patterns that I usually look for because they're easy to spot and easy to trade. But remember, every thing I'm going to say here is within the context of something I said in chapter 3. Let me refresh your memory:

> Chapter 3 excerpt
>
> *But if the stock is still in play because the 1 minute chart is showing strength and green candles forming and the five minute chart is showing strength and*

*green candles forming, I start to watch the level 2 closely for huge position size sellers as well as the 1 minute chart to see about me taking the trade and getting a good entry point. This is nuts and bolts of my trading strategy...*

## First chart pattern - The Squeeze Up One Minute Micro Pullback

This is one of my favorite chart patterns to trade. The way it usually forms is a stock gradually starts increasing in price but not enough to gain a lot of attention from other traders because it hasn't begun to make new high of day prices yet. But if you are watching the scanner you will notice the gradual increase and price activity. If you're following my strategy you will already have the stock's charts already loaded up waiting for the break out as well as having the ticker loaded on your Robinhood app. What happens next is where the fun begins. The stock's price starts to really increase because now other traders have notice the price squeezing up and jumped in causing higher price action. Once some of those trader make a little a profit they will begin to sell their positions. This will cause the price to pullback a little (Micro pullback). Here is my and your opportunity.

Check where the price fell from (the latest high) and that's your entry (you have to be fast). You take the trade as the price begins coming back up to the point. Traders who missed that first squeeze up will be buying at this point. This is the first pullback. Once you have confirmation that you got filled, IMMEDIATELY prepare your limit sell order that is seven to ten cents above your average price. Once the price reaches this point or about to reach this point submit your order to sell and take your profits. But, if the price goes against you, you may have to cancel your previous order if it was already submitted and then retype your new limit order price which is the downside to this strategy because as you are canceling and typing the price maybe falling deeper. Another strategy you could use after your order is filled is IMMEDIATELY prepared your limit sell order ten cents below your average price. The reason for this is Robinhood (as of this writing) doesn't have hot keys [keyboard commands that allow traders to enter and exit trades very fast] and stock prices can fluctuate very quickly and in the event the stock price falls against you, you want to be ready to submit your order to stop the loss. On the flip side to this, if the stock price goes in your favor (let's say a 15 to 20 cents increase) you can still submit your already prepared order and the Robinhood app will do its best to get you filled at your limit order price or better. And since you submitted your order when the current price was up at least 15 cents that's where the Robinhood app is trying to get you filled.

> *For example: if I prepare a limit sell order to sell at $1.95 and my average share price was $2.05 and the stock price rises to $2.17, if I submit my prepared limit sell order of $1.95 while the stock price is up at $2.17 I will get filled at $2.17 not $1.95. Why? Because Robinhood takes your limit sell orders and tries to sell your shares at the set limit price or a price better if the stock is up.*

The downside is you may get filled at lower price than you wish. The app tries to get you filled at the best price but it's not perfect. Additionally, with both of these strategies you could sell half or ¾ of your position and hold the rest in hopes of higher price movement (in the event the price went in your favor and increased) to capture more profits.

This is one of my favorite strategies because stocks are very volatile and sometimes you could have gotten in at a good price but the stock doesn't get good follow through and doesn't hold the price levels and/or never reaches your profit target price before it starts to reverse. The great thing is with this strategy you're well prepared and ready to stop the loss if the stock continues to fall towards your exit price and in this example it was $1.95.

If you happen to miss this opportunity on the first micro pullback you can continue to watch the stock and price action and get in on the second mirco pullback. But again, you must be quick with the buy and sell triggers. Remember to prepare your seven to ten cent below average price limit sell order immediately after you get filled.

Finally, if you miss the second micro pullback you have to wait for the stock to consolidate and set up again. DO NOT TRADE THE THIRD MICRO PULLBACK. By this time the stock is usually too extended off its moving average and set to fall back down and either reverse or trade side ways.

## Second chart pattern - Bull Flags

Sometimes stocks move up so quickly that traders aren't fast enough to profit and take advantage of the move with low risk. They either have to look for another trade or let the trade pullback and form a bull flag and set up again.

## What is a bull flag?

A bull flag pattern is formed when a stock moves up in three or more consecutive green candles then falls back about 3 or more red candles with each red candle achieving a newer low price. Then a green candle forms and if the green candle surpasses the previous candle's high price whether that previous candle is red or green that's your opportunity to buy with your profit target 10 or 20 cents from your entry and your exit price being the low price of the previous candle. The reason I say whether the previous candle is red or green is because as the stock price begins to reverse to the long side a green candle may form but it may not surpass the previous candle's high price. So, though the bull flag has formed you don't have your entry point until your current green candle makes a new high from the lows.

## Third chart pattern – T5/Circuit Breaker halt of a rising price

The way hunters search for game is the way traders search for volatility and sometimes massive volatility causes insane price action of a particular stock. This price action may be upwards or downward but for this particular chart pattern I pay a attention to the up swing. If a stock rises 10% or more within a five minute period it will be put on a T5/ Circuit breaker halt. This means that all trading for this particular stock will be ceased for a period of five or ten minutes allowing traders to gather themselves through this frenzy. No one can buy or sell shares of this stock until the halt is finished. The reason why I like this pattern is because the super-fast rise in the stock's price which caused the circuit breaker halt indicates a lot of buyers and buying means higher price action.

The way you trade this pattern is two ways and each way had it's benefits and disadvantages: The first way is this. Buy the stock as you would any other stock that's showing strength and rising price activity. If you are holding your position as the price rises into a T5/circuit breaker halt during the halt prepare to sell half or all of your entire position when the stock resumes trading. Reason being, many times after a halt and the stocks resumes they tend to resume at much higher prices than when they were halted

(Bringing you more profit) but that new higher price doesn't always hold and they tend to fall very fast because so many buyers immediately start selling their positions. Also, they can resume at much lower prices than they were before the halt so you must be ready. If you are still holding you may end up easily taking a loss. But, due to the high volatility the stock does sometimes rise back up making new highs and that can be your exit point there.

The second way is this. If you missed the upward price action before the T5/Circuit breaker halt, while the stock is halted you can prepare your entry order to get in when the stock resumes. If it resumes lower than what it was or a little higher than what it was when it was halted, make your entry point the price where it was halted or that new open price. And since its not far off the halt price the attention of other traders on this stock after it reopened tend to cause it to squeeze back up pass the original halt price allowing you to grab some quick profits. Just don't hold too long, take your profits and get out. If it resumes a lot higher than what it was when it was halted, you could either jump right in regardless of where the price is for fear of missing out on a major upward swing or don't trade the stock at all and wait for it to set up again to reduce your risk.

## Last chart pattern - Red to Green Move

This pattern I trade the least of the four because of the way it sets up. The trader must be quick and ready to sell once their profit target is hit.

A red to green move pattern forms when a stock that had all the signs pre-market that it should increase in price during the first 10 to 15 minutes of opening bell but the exact opposite happens. The stock price falls tremendously say 20 to 50 cents maybe more showing a long or consecutive red candles. Sometimes the stock never recovers that day and stays red trading sideways with small green candles but not enough for any smart trader to buy into. But other times the stock price may fall 20 to 50 cents maybe more showing a long or consecutive red candles but in a quick change of sentiment, green candles start to form and the stock price begins to increase even to the point that it begins approaching the high of day price point. This is your entry point - the high of day price point. Take the trade, prepare your seven to ten cents below average price limit sell order and sell if your profit target is hit or sell if your exit price is hit.

There are other chart patterns that traders look for but I don't particularly trade them. As I stated earlier in the book, my primary focus is to teach you the strategies that I use everyday to profit as a day trader. There is no need for me to give you a comprehensive guide to day trading because there are numerous books on the market that will do that for you.

## Chapter 6: HOW TO TRADE WITH SCANNERS

If there was any tool within my repertoire that I absolutely cannot day trade on Robinhood without it would be my stock scanner. I'm able to find the stocks that I do because of it. Here I'm going tell you about the stock scanner that I use every day and how I set them up to find those hot stocks that I trade.

The scanner that I use is the scanner within the think or swim trading platform. I like this scanner mainly because what other scanners do for a monthly charge, this does relatively the same thing for free.

The way I set my scanners are like this:
I set my price scanner to only find me stocks priced between $1 and $20

I set my volume scanner to only find me stocks with intraday volume of 100,000 to 50,000,000

I set my percent change scanner to +4% to find me stocks that gapped up at least 4% or more

I set my float scanner to find me stocks with floats under 20,000,000

These are the criteria I set within my scanners and every day they bring me back stocks that fit these parameters.

## Chapter 7: TRADE MANAGEMENT AND TRADING PSYCHOLOGY

Its been said by a many of traders that day trading is not easy but it is simple. I concur. But, what I will add is if you ever embarked on becoming a successful day trader it will be one of the hardest things you'll ever do. Why? Because every trader loves to watch money flow easy into their account and hates it when they're losing money. And this is when trading psychology enters the picture. Most beginner traders are excited about trading and making fast money. But it's this emotional high that blinds them to the reality and downside of trading; losing money, in other words - red days.

The first time you take a trade and you lose money it may feel like someone burst your happy balloon. So, to return to a happy place you might rush and take another trade in hopes you will make money on that trade, and if you do that's great. But chances are you'll lose money and now you're no longer thinking clear, your mental state is tainted and your emotions are getting the best of you. Again, this is called revenge trading and its never a good outcome. I've been and many other traders have been infected by this at one time or another because when a trade goes against you unexpectedly is frustrating.

But the truth is no trader knows what a stock might do from one tick to the next. You must be prepared for the upswings and the downswings. There are so many emotions that can color your ability to trade objectively and here are a few:

**Greed** - After picking a couple of winning trades, or getting into a trade and watching the price run up, greed can cause this situation to go from good to bad very fast. How? By holding onto the trade too long hoping the price goes higher and you make more money. But, what usually happens is the price takes a quick turn downwards and now what was once a winning trade is now a losing trade and you feel like the dummy.

**Fear** - This one comes into play when you see an opportunity to take a trade and all your analysis show that the trade has a high probable chance of moving in your favor and you don't take the trade because of fear. You stand on the sidelines and watch the trade move without you. And whaddayouknow it did move in your favor.

**FOMO - SHORT FOR Fear Of Missing Out**

This happens as you're watching the market you see a stock spiking upwards fast. You quickly start to feel like every one getting a piece of this action except you. So instead of waiting for the stock to consolidate and set up again you jump In as fast as you can and what happens! The stock reverses and falls just as fast as it spiked and now your taking a huge lost. What might even happen is that huge loss might even turn bigger because the stock reversed so fast it really threw you off and instead of selling your position and taking the huge loss, you hold onto the stock hoping it moves back up but it doesn't. It just falls even further making your loss bigger.

**FOBW - Fear Of Being Wrong**

This happens when you don't take a trade not because of the possibility of losing money but fear that the trade will not be what you expected. But again, no trader knows with absolute certainty what direction a stock price will move. Successful traders watch trends, chart pattern and other technical analysis that help make trading decision.

There are other emotions you will experience during your trading career that impact your ability to trade well but I won't cover them here. Read a comprehensive guide or blog to day trading and you'll learn those.

## Managing Your Trades

The best traders have learn to manage their trades well. They do their best to trade objectively without their emotions clouding their better judgement. They've learned to be patient and let the market dictate how they will trade daily. They enter the market with a strategy and wait for good set ups to form and give them the greatest probable chance of success. And once they are in trades they don't sell to early due to fear of loss,  and they don't hold too long due to greed.

## Chapter 8: CREATING A TRADING PLAN

As a beginner trader I created a month to month trading plan to help gradually increase my confidence, manage my risk tolerance and to build up metrics. You should do the same. Use these plans exactly the way they are or modify them a little to help fit your personal situation.

**Your first month:**

This month you shouldn't trade with real money. Open a paper trading account at one of the various trading platform brokerages out there and start to work on the strategies I use and laid out earlier or begin to develop your own. Strive to trade as close to your situation as possible. For example, if you plan to start trading with an $1000 cash account when you paper trade, trade with only a $1000 account balance. Try to profit everyday and finish green daily. Take that $1000 turn it into $2000 by the end of the month. Take only one to two trades a day and if you lose $50 to $100 in a day you're done for that day. Come back fresh the next trading day.

## 2nd Month:

Repeat month 1 if you are still not profitable or not comfortable yet trading real money. But if you successfully passed month 1 standards then move to this:

Start trading with real money. $1000 cash Try to turn this into $2000. Take only one to three trades a day and if you lose $100 in a day you're done for that day. Come back fresh the next trading day. Your daily goal is $100 a day with a accuracy rating of at least 50%. Your weekly goal should $300 to $500.

## 3rd Month:

Repeat month 2 if you are still not comfortable yet moving on the bigger risk. But if you are ready move on a little:

One to three trades a day with daily profit of $200 a day. Your weekly goal is $600 to $1000. With a accuracy rating of 60% to 70%. If you lose $200 during any single day you're done for that day. Come back the next trading day. If you are able to consistently reach your weekly goals this month you are on pace for 30k to 50k a year.

**4th Month:**

Repeat month 3 if you are not comfortable moving on to bigger risk. But if you are ready, move to this:

One to three trades a day with daily profit of $400 a day. Your weekly goal is $1200 to $2000. With a accuracy rating of 70% to 80%. If you lose $400 during any single day you're done for that day. Come back the next trading day. If you are able to consistently reach your weekly goals this month you are on pace for 62k to 104k a year.

**5th Month:**

Repeat month 4 if you are not comfortable moving on to bigger risk. But, if you are ready, move to this:

One to three trades a day with daily profit of $800 a day. Your weekly goal is $2400 to $4000. With a accuracy rating of 70% to 80%. If you lose $800 during any single day you're done for that day. Come back the next trading day. If you are able to consistently reach your weekly goals this month you are on pace for 124k to 208k a year.

**6th Month:**

Repeat month 5 if you are not comfortable moving on to bigger risk. But, if you are ready, move to this:

One to three trades a day with daily profit of $1000 a day. Your weekly goal is $3000 to $5000. With a accuracy rating of 80% to 90%. If you lose $1000 during any single day you're done for that day. Come back the next trading day. If you are able to consistently reach your weekly goals this month you are on pace for 156k to 260k a year.

Follow these trading plans and get yourself to the next level of time and money freedom.

Thank you for reading

Peace

MIKE H.

## Day Trading Tools

- Laptop or Desktop computer (One or two additional monitors to watch more than one stock [optional]
- A brokerage firm (The company that submits your buy and sell orders, keeps records of your financial transactions, and connects you to the stock market)
    - Here are some options
        - Lightspeed ($25,000 minimum, Located within the United States, PDT Rule restricted, have to pay commissions on every trade, and customizable hot keys for getting in and out of trades fast)
        - Speedtrader ($25,000 minimum, Located within the United States, PDT Rule restricted, have to pay commissions on every trade, customizable hot keys for getting in and out of trades fast)

- Suretrader ($500 minimum, Located outside the United States, Not restricted by PDT Rule, have to pay commissions on every trade, customizable hot keys for getting in and out of trades fast)
- Tradezero ($1000 minimum, Located outside the United States, Not restricted by PDT Rule, have to pay commissions on every trade, Not available to USA residents)
- TD ameritrade ($50 minimum Located within the United States, PDT Rule restricted on margin accounts, no commissions on trades, limited hot keys) **THIS IS THE BROKER I USE**
- Robin hood (No minimum, Located within the United States, PDT Rule restricted, no commissions on trades, no hot keys, available on mobile device and desktop) **THIS IS THE BROKER I USE**

**Here is the website:**
http://share.robinhood.com/michaeh737

Charting Software

Here are few options
- E-signal
- Ninja trader
- Google
- Think or swim (**THIS IS THE SOFTWARE I USE**)
- Das Trader

A tradervue account to track your trades

## Glossary

**Cash account** - When you trade in cash account, the amount of money in the account is exactly the same as how much you deposited. When you take a trade, you have to wait T+3 (Transaction + 3 days to settle). Stocks take 3 days for transactions to settle. It's like waiting for a check to clear.

**Day Trading** – The activity of buying and selling shares of a stock intraday (same day)

**Float** – The number of outstanding shares a company has available to trade.

**Green day** – Day Trading jargon for a day when you've made money after you finished trading for the day.

**Margin account** - margin account requires a margin agreement. With a margin account trades still take T+3, but instead of requiring you to wait 3 days before you can trade with that money, the broker gives you credit to trade with the money as soon as the trade has been completed. This is what allows day traders to take 10+ trades in a single morning. We can trade the same cash 1000x times a day if we'd like. All we need is a margin account.

**Paper Trading** – Is the activity of using fake money to simulate the purchase of shares of stock during real or delayed trading times.

**Pattern Day Trader Rules -** The Pattern Day Trader (PDT) Rule states that if a trader takes 3 or more day trades in a 5 day period, they are a day trader and they must maintain a minimum account balance of $25,000 USD.

**Position size** – The amount of shares of stock you purchased

**Stock Market Hours -** The market is open from 9:30am -4pm EST Monday –Friday. There are holidays when the market is closed or closes at 1pm. Pre-market and after-hours trading is available but liquidity is often very low because there aren't a lot of buyers or sellers trading after hours.

**Red day** – Day Trading jargon for a day when you've lost money after you finished trading for the day.

www.ingramcontent.com/pod-product-compliance
Lightning Source LLC
Chambersburg PA
CBHW030500220526
45464CB00006B/2593